JESUS

vs

I0087495

satan

Josh Burris

Team JESUS Collection

Aurora, Colorado

Josh Burris/Team JESUS Collection
Aurora, Colorado

Unless otherwise indicated, all Scripture quotations are from the *Holy Bible*, King James Version.

Book Layout © 2017 BookDesignTemplates.com

Graphic Credits
Photography by: pixabayimage/Donterase, iStockphoto/Fergregory and pixabayimage/Mediengestalter
Book Cover Designer, Adrian White
PENTPROGraphics – www.psalmistpro.com

JESUS vs satan / Josh Burris. – 1st ed.
ISBN-13: 978-0692121351

Team JESUS

Eternal Life Roster
God
Jesus
Holy Spirit
Angels
Believers

Vs

Team satan

Eternal Death Roster
satan
sin
flesh
demons
non-believers

Whose Team are you on?

If you're not exactly sure or you have
even the slightest doubt, don't wait!
Find out now.

Scene Selection

How to find scriptures in the Bible

For the purpose of this book, it is important to know how to find the Bible scriptures referenced in this book so you can read them. There are different translations. Some reliable ones are *The King James Version, The New King James Version, The Amplified Bible* and *New American Standard Bible.*

The Bible comprises 66 Books divided into two main sections known as the Old Testament and New Testament. Read the next paragraph to see how to find a Bible verse in your Bible.

An example of a scripture reference is **John 3:16-17,** John is the name of the Bible Book. The "3" before the colon refers to the third chapter of John and the "16-17" after the colon refers to verses 16 through 17 of that chapter. In most Bibles, verse numbers typically appear in superscript format. Here are these two verses:

[16] *"For God so loved the world, that He gave His only begotten Son, that whoever believes in Him shall not perish, but have eternal life.* [17] *For God did not send*

the Son into the world to judge the world, but that the world might be saved through Him" (NASB).

The Book of John is in the New Testament. If you were to just see **John 3**, that would mean turn to the book of John, find chapter 3 and read the whole chapter (since no specific verses were given).

Now you are ready to look up books, chapters and verses in your Bible! As you read this book, please look up the Bible verses referenced so you can see what the Scriptures say for yourself.

Attention Smartphone users!
There are a number of free, easy to use Bible apps such as *YouVersion, Bible by Olive Tree,* and *Blue Letter Bible.* See which one(s) you like the best.

<u>Special Note for the Reader</u>

Please leave all preconceived notions here <u>before</u> you continue and be sure to read the whole book from beginning to end. Now go ahead and get started.

Book Trailer

This book introduces the most important matchup in the entire world, ***JESUS vs satan.*** These teams will *never* join together. It really is this simple. No matter who you are or where you are from, every single person in the world *is* a team member of one of these two teams.

Out of everything you could possibly think of in life, *nothing* is more important than knowing *which* team you are on. Some may be surprised to hear this… However, if you have been searching for truth in a chaotic world, this is it.

The following questions are important to consider if you have never given them any serious thought.

Have you ever wondered, what happens when I die?
Who is Jesus and what did He do for me?
Who is satan and how can he ruin my life?
How is it that every single person in the world belongs only to one of these two teams?

The answers are here. Let's take a closer look at both teams.

satan's team - Eternal Death

The roster for the **Losing team** includes **satan, sin, flesh, demons and non-believers.**

It is important to know satan (formerly called Lucifer when he was in heaven), was created by God. He was a holy angel, "the anointed cherub" (Ezekiel 28:14). He was adorned with every precious jewel imaginable (Ezekiel 28:13) and was "perfect" in beauty and in all his ways from the day of his creation until iniquity was found in him (Ezekiel 28:15). **Iniquity** means – sin, wickedness, evil.

Satan became prideful and arrogant in his beauty, power and status. Though he is an angel, satan had "free will" just like we do. He wanted to be God and thought he could overthrow God saying, "I will ascend into heaven, I will exalt my throne above the stars of God" (Isaiah 14:13-14). Because of his rebellion, God cast him out of heaven. His pride came at a high cost. God is sovereign, He alone sits on the throne and all Glory belongs to Him.

Satan is entirely opposed to God and does every-thing in his power to keep <u>every</u> person from knowing God. His plan involves doing whatever it takes to make all people worship him. The name "satan" means, "ad-versary." This means satan is God's adversary, he is against God. Anyone on satan's team is against God. No one on satan's team can defeat him; he manipulates and rules those who are on his team. However, it is crucial to know he is a **defeated** enemy of God and always will be.

Simply put, **sin** is anything that rebels against the known will of God or transgresses the law of God (1 John 3:4). **Transgression** means – wrongdoing or a vio-lation of a law. Sin is the result of rebellion. **Satan's main strategy is to get us to sin to separate us from God for eternity just like him.**

For example, when it comes to driving, there are laws to follow. Speeding is against the law. If you are traveling on a highway where the speed limit is 55 miles per hour and you pass a police officer on the highway while going 80 miles per hour, you have violated a law. The police officer will turn on his lights, pursue you and pull you over. In this case, you would receive a speeding ticket.

Read this carefully. In this scenario, speeding represents **sin**. The laws for driving represent God's boundaries to keep you out of trouble. If you follow the laws, God will take care of you. Now, satan wants you to rebel, to sin against God. **This is not a game for satan, he actually wants every person in the world on his team.**

This brings us to a point where we have to make a choice. If you rebel, the result is sin. The sin is the consequence. This is why the cop pulled you over and you received a speeding ticket. This is a big deal because one consequence can be life changing and lead to more trouble.

For example, because of the ticket, you were late to work. Since you were late to work, your boss fired you. Now you need to find a new job and so on. If you had been going 55 miles per hour, you would not have been pulled over by a cop. There would not be a speeding ticket to pay for. You would have made it to work on time and would still have your job.

The bottom line is there are consequences for violating laws. **Rebellion leads to sin**. The consequence for sin is that it separates us from God; it breaks our relationship with Him. This is a universal problem; this concerns everyone who is <u>not</u> perfect. This includes the "good person." Every person is guilty of sin and no one is exempt. **Romans 3:23 says,** *"For all have sinned and come short of the glory of God."* For our relationship with God to be restored, our problem with sin must be addressed.

Remember this: sin has a price and <u>must</u> be paid for.

Flesh refers to the sinful and selfish nature we are all born with. The works of the flesh are evident. A few of them are sexual immorality, sensuality, idolatry, sorcery, jealousy, drunkenness, orgies and more (see Galatians 5:19-21). Works of the flesh do not have to be as apparent as these; they can be more subtle and turn into something more serious very quickly.

The flesh has a rebellious nature so fighting against the flesh is not only crucial but it is something we must <u>learn</u>. A young child doesn't need to learn how to behave badly but they *do* need to learn *good* behavior. After learning, we must choose to behave well. We must choose to do right instead of wrong. Therefore, fighting the flesh is a daily battle. We can best learn what is right and what is wrong from God.

Demons (often referred to as fallen angels) are angels that satan convinced to join him in his rebellion against God (Revelation 12:9). Demons can possess non-believers. <u>Possess</u> means – take control of somebody so the person's behavior and/or thinking are affected. They can cause physical ailment or physical impairment, personality changes, convulsions, superhuman strength and more.

Because demons are spiritual beings, they are capable of possessing human bodies (only non-believers). The Bible gives examples of people who were possessed by demons. You can see one in Luke 4:33-36. Since demons follow satan, they obey his commands.

A non-believer is anyone who does <u>not</u> believe in Jesus and does <u>not</u> accept the free gift of Salvation that only comes through Jesus. A non-believer chooses to rebel against God and continually lives in sin. They choose, whether knowingly or unknowingly, to be responsible for paying for their own sins. It is very important to know and understand *"the wages of sin is death"* (Romans 6:23). This means a non-believer will pay the full penalty of sin, which is **death**.

Death means - Eternal Separation from God, or
Eternal death.

Adam and Eve were the first two humans God
created and they were perfect (Genesis 2:7, 2:21-23).
They had perfect communion with God. This means they
had a perfect relationship. God told Adam there was one
thing he must not do. Genesis 2:16-17 reads:

*16 The LORD God commanded the man, saying,
"From any tree of the garden you may eat freely; 17 but
from the tree of the knowledge of good and evil you shall
not eat, for in the day that you eat from it you will surely
die." (NASB)*

In this context, "surely die" means **Eternal
death.** Satan, appearing in the form of a serpent, tempted
Adam and Eve to sin and succeeded (Genesis 3:1-7).
Verses 4 and 5 put two of satan's favorite weapons on
display, lying and deceiving. Genesis 3: 4-5:

*4 The serpent said to the woman, "You surely will
not die! 5 For God knows that in the day you eat from it
your eyes will be opened, and you will be like God,
knowing good and evil."*

Adam had a choice: to obey or rebel against God. Ultimately, he **chose** to rebel. Adam's rebellion towards God resulted in bringing the consequences of sin into the world. Even the pain of child birth that women go through is a consequence of Adam and Eve's choice to rebel (Genesis 3:16). **God means exactly what He says.**

Since we are Adam's descendants, we have inherited sin from him (Romans 5:12-19). Therefore, sin has been passed down through the seed of man to every generation of mankind. **This means we are all born into sin, everyone starts on satan's team as non-believers by default.**

Satan was the first to rebel against God and he lost his position in heaven forever as a result.

Satan schemes ways for man to "give in" to his way of life and "ignore" the way God wants us to live. Satan wants every person to be like him, against God. He hates God and he hates every person. **Yes, this means satan hates you.**

However, satan could not foresee that God had a plan. This plan involves the **"The Gospel"** which means the "Good News" and it contains **God's Truth** (much more on this later). Satan hates this plan and makes it his business to keep people from knowing this truth at all cost.

If we choose to live in rebellion and reject God, satan's team is the one we stay on.

Our Enemy

Satan, (also known as the devil), and demons know more facts about Jesus than any person. They know exactly who Jesus is; they used to live in Heaven with Him! They know the meaning of Jesus' death, His resurrection and the truth of the scriptures (James 2:19). Satan knows that his power and time is limited (Revelation 12:12). His mission is **"to steal, kill and destroy"** every person (John 10:10).

Satan is the "Primary Source" behind every false world religion, cult, false teacher and false god.

Disorder comes from satan. He wants to keep every person from the truth. This is the reason the world has its own definition of what religion means. If you Google the word "Religion," more than 400 million results will pop up! Can you see that satan is trying to hide **Truth**? There should be 1 result that pops up.

Religion has one purpose: to restore our relationship with God because sin separated us from Him.

The word "Religion" does not scare satan; he uses it to manipulate many people into worshipping him. It is very important to know that satan desires to be worshipped and will go to great lengths to accomplish this.

Remember the lie he told Adam and Eve, that they would "<u>not</u>" surely die and that they would be like God. **Never** forget that satan rebelled against God and became an enemy of God for Eternity. Make no mistake, satan will do anything he can think of to make you an enemy of God for eternity, just like he is.

Religion is not the reason for wars. The first murder occurred from uncontrolled anger. Cain murdered his brother Able (See Genesis 4:1-8). Religion had nothing to do with Cain killing his brother. There was no war. God warned Cain that "sin" was looking for an opportunity to overtake him and that he had to master it. It was Cain who chose to give in to sin. Cain sinned against God by killing his brother Able. Cain did not love his brother Able.

If every single person (starting with Adam and Eve) obeyed God, the world would not know war. God did not create us so He could have a front row seat to watch us kill each other. Rebellion towards God comes at a high price. Disobeying God is like sitting at home with all the doors unlocked. This is an open invitation for satan and sin to walk right through any door. Who locks the doors or leaves the doors unlocked in your home? You do!

In any area of your life, you choose whether to lock satan out or let him come in.

One of satan's plans to keep people from God is to offer "other options" or "alternatives" otherwise known as **lies**. This is why there are so many religions. How do you know which religion to choose? Some of them may look or sound good, their purpose is only to cause confusion. So many religions make it seem like there are more than just two teams doesn't it? **Do not let this fool you, there are only two teams and this will never change.** False World religions and false gods come from satan and those on his team.

Remember this: Categories of religion only exist to hide the truth.

It is important to understand that satan tries to imitate God. In doing so, he has used men to cause mass confusion. In fact, satan wants everyone to praise and worship him. Some people do this proudly. **However, many others worship satan unknowingly, not just hundreds, thousands or millions but billions of people.**

There are several different ways satan works to achieve this. He understands that many people are <u>not</u> drawn to darkness but to light. **He is <u>not</u> an ugly red, idiotic angelic being with horns and a pitchfork as the world portrays him. He is not a Halloween character.**

Though satan was cast out of heaven, his appearance has not changed. He is still "perfect in beauty" but he is the <u>most</u> evil, demonic being in existence. 2 Corinthians 11:14 tells us, "satan disguises himself as an angel of light," this warns us that he is the master of deception.

This is such an important **truth** to understand. **Sin** can be "disguised" as something that looks good, which can make us think it is something we want or need. A "god" or "idol" can be a person, like a favorite athlete or singer/rapper. A god can be a sports team, job, money, fetish, statue, or graven image. These are just a few examples of false gods or idols. An **idol** is defined as: an image or representation of a god used as an object of worship. **In reality, satan is the god many people choose to worship.**

Worshipping a person or a sport can entertain you and get you to spend money. But many people do not know the person they worship personally, there is no relationship. For some people money is their god. Working 70-80 hours a week is more important than anyone or anything else. **Everyone** worships something.

Consider this question. How does seeing your favorite football team, singer or whatever you worship get rid of sin? It does not. Maybe all the hours you spend at work to make money can help. No, money cannot pay for sin. Here is the point, if you haven't been concerned about what you worship, now you should be. **There is no idol or false god that can solve your sin problem and get you right with God.** Exodus 20:3 tells us, *"You shall have no other gods before Me."* (NASB). How much more clear can God be?

False teachers are non-believers who cause confusion. They represent false gods of **man-made**

religions which means satan has manipulated these men for his purposes. They spread lies and sometimes try to mix in certain truths. This is satan's way of trying to "blend in" which makes things "as clear as mud." Some may even claim they know Jesus but they are really impostors. They can deceive other people by having attractive characteristics and appearing to have good morals.

False teachers may seem knowledgeable about the Bible. They can be Pastors in churches and even have a program on television. **Jesus warns us about false teachers** (read Matthew 23:1-29). Also, 1 John 4:2-3 tells us:

"By this you know the Spirit of God: every spirit that confesses that Jesus Christ has come in the flesh is from God; and every spirit that does not confess Jesus is not from God; this is the spirit of the antichrist, of which you have heard that it is coming, and now it is already in the world" (NASB).

Be aware that satan or anyone on his team may try disguising themselves by acting as if they are on Jesus' team. Be careful that you are not fooled by external appearances.

Think of your favorite candy and the kind of wrapper or packaging it comes in when you first buy it. Maybe you like the color(s) too. Nevertheless, when you open it, the candy does not change into a healthy snack. The candy is still sugar. It is bad for you, can make you sick, give you cavities, etc.

In some ways, sugar is similar to sin. It can look good and taste good but is only temporary. Sugar has long-term effects; it destroys the body in many ways. Sugar kills people. **Sin** is much worse than sugar; it takes us away from God and makes us vulnerable to satan's attacks. Without God, satan will beat you to a pulp and leave you in ruin. Sin destroys the body, mind and soul. This is what satan wants for you. Sin kills people too but not temporarily, it leads to **Eternal Death.**

Even though satan knows **there is only one God**, he is able to deceive many people into believing in false gods or that God does not exist. **God stands alone and He tells us exactly who He is.** Deuteronomy 4:39 says:

"Know therefore today, and take it to your heart, that the LORD, He is God in heaven above and on earth below; there is no other" (NASB).

That's just one verse, there are several. God is very clear on this matter. **How many times does God have to say, "There are no other gods besides Me" for us to understand what He means by that?** Since *it is* God telling us, **one** time should be *more* than enough.

The real question is, do you believe what God is telling you about Himself? That He is exactly who He says He is. In Isaiah 42:8, God says, *"I am the LORD, that is My name; I will not give My glory to another, Nor My praise to graven images."* **God tells us exactly what He created in Genesis 1, He did not create any other god(s).** God does <u>not</u> share His glory.

God cannot be cloned or replicated, period.

You may have seen a sign or bumper sticker on a car that says, *"Tolerance"* or *"Coexist"* that is spelled using symbols associated with religions. These **two** words foster the idea that there are multiple "gods" and religions. This makes it seem like everyone can choose from a wide variety of **"custom made"** gods and religions. And if it suits you, choose none. To each his own, sound familiar? Just be respectful and be accepting. That sounds good right?

This is exactly what satan intended. Just one problem, these two words **actually suggest** that we all **rebel against God** and **obey satan**. This is one lie satan has been using for a very long time, many people are deceived by this lie.

Understand this, satan thinks it is easy to get people to worship him. Because of him there are over 4,000 religions and too many false gods to count. Is this really all it takes to keep billions of people in rebellion towards God? Satan disguises himself in the form of "false gods" and "false world religions" to get **you** to worship him. Still sound good?

If you believe there is another god, it is a false god and you know where you stand. **You do not believe God's Truth but you believe satan's lies instead.** You are responsible for choosing what you believe. No one else can choose for you, it's YOUR choice. This is "Free will." There are only two options to choose from, **God's Truth or satan's lies.**

God speaks about those who don't believe in Him. Psalm 14:1 says, *"The fool has said in his heart, there is no God."*

Satan will gladly tell you the lie that God does not exist. Then he will laugh at you for believing him because he <u>knows</u> God. A person, who decides they do not believe in God for whatever reason, makes one thing perfectly clear. That they openly declare they are on satan's team. This person may say, "I don't believe in satan either." This pleases satan just the same, he's greedy and will take you anyway.

Truth: No one has to believe in satan to be on his team.

Satan wants us to think that he is good and willing to give us anything we want if we worship him. Please understand this. Yes, satan actually has a game plan of his own to fool every person. Maybe you didn't know this until right now.

False gods and false religions deceive people who rebel and reject God (1 Timothy 4:1-2). All false gods, false world religions and cults consist of non-believers who belong to satan's team. **In this world, billions of people worship satan as their god.** Some non-believers are unaware that they are on satan's team.

For example, terrorists who plan to kill themselves and murder other people in the process may <u>think</u> they were instructed to do so by a god they worship.

However, they **do not** know satan has deceived them. They actually worship a false god, which means they worship satan and they are on his team.

In Exodus 20:13 God says, "*You shall not murder*" (NASB). This is one of the ten commandments and is still relevant today. **Jesus does not** have any team members that go around blowing themselves up and murdering people in His name. In **John 8:44**, Jesus tells us satan was a murderer from the beginning, has no truth in him and that "he is a liar and the father of lies."

Evil is a person, not a thing. Evil is extremely personal, it only exists in this world in persons. Think about this for a minute. A tree is not evil. Grass is not evil. A mountain is not evil. However, *it is* true that satan *is* evil and <u>always</u> will be. A person who murders another person is evil. They are obedient to satan and an adversary of God. But this person could decide to change and obey God instead.

Love is a person, it does not exist outside of persons. Flowers do not love. Water does not love. Food does not love. However, it is true that God loves and that He *is* love which is the only reason love exist (more on this later). God is <u>not</u> evil and is <u>not</u> capable of being evil.

To satan, it does not matter whether you know you are on his team or not. He is happy as long as you are NOT on Jesus' team.

What kind of people are on satan's team? We can get a glimpse from 2 Timothy 3:1-4:

"But realize this, that in the last days difficult times will come. For men will be lovers of self, lovers of money, boastful, arrogant, revilers, disobedient to parents, ungrateful, unholy, unloving, irreconcilable, malicious gossips, without self-control, brutal, haters of good, treacherous, reckless, conceited, lovers of pleasure rather than lovers of God" (NASB).

Let's simplify this, satan has created many ways for people to worship him as if he were a god. He wants to keep you and every person on his team forever. Make no mistake, satan is serious about his mission and he works hard to imitate God. **He's certainly not lacking in the "effort" department.** He has many "disguises" and wears many "different hats".

There is more to this plan so pay attention. For a long time satan has been working to make more and more religions. Now there are more religions than ever. There has been major growth but these religions are merely distractions. What's the end result? There are more people rejecting God than ever.

In addition, more people than ever are showing that they do not fear God. In fact, in these days, many people think there are many ways or paths to God. **However, this is a lie.**

There is only One Way to God; it's Jesus.

Right now, there are millions of false gods to spread across all the false world religions but eventually this number will change. **All false gods and false world religions will become one, there will only be one false god, false world religion and a one world government.**

This is all a part of satan's larger plan, that all people worship him. **This means a great number of people in this world will worship satan.** This is one of his ultimate goals; he <u>never</u> stops trying to be "like" God. Take this warning seriously. **There are <u>not</u> thousands of teams; <u>only</u> the two teams in this book.**

Some people reading this book will find out they are on satan's team but <u>don't</u> have to stay on **satan's losing team**. Some lives will be changed forever because this is a **"Wake-up call"**. Some people will be sick and tired of being on satan's team and will join **Jesus' winning team**. This will be something worth sharing with others, angels in Heaven rejoice when even one person leaves satan's team!

One thing satan hates, people leaving his team. Though he really tried, he couldn't stop this book from being written or printed. **This book was written to ensure that satan <u>will</u> lose team members.**

Please know this:
Rejecting God does have consequences.
Let this be a warning to anyone reading this book.

Satan <u>will</u> play you for a fool if you let him. He does not feel shame. Remember, satan attempts to imitate God. Don't take this lightly because many people *are* fooled by his schemes. Satan is full of darkness, he has no potential for good and there is no light or truth in him.

Has satan tricked you into worshipping him by disguising himself as a false god or within a false world religion?

Satan works overtime hours to tempt us. Giving in to temptation is what gives birth to sin. He wants us to see sin as harmless fun that is appealing and pleasant. Take a minute to think about how this happens in your own life. Temptation is the vehicle that "sin" travels in.

This vehicle may run well and have incredible horsepower, going from 0-50 mph in 3 seconds. Of course, it has tinted windows and shines perfectly on the outside. Know what could be inside the car *before* you open the door. Be aware that ruin and devastation can be hiding in this car.

There is no question, you <u>will</u> see cars driving by or approaching from around the corner. You might even see people you know in some of these cars. Do not open the door and get in the wrong car. A car could represent stealing, lying, taking or selling drugs, etc. Sin is selfish and does not care about your life or anyone else's life.

Sin will ruin your life and the lives of those close to you. It spreads like a disease or a virus.

Remember this: temptation can look good but will always leave you feeling empty and dissatisfied.

In 2016, a television show called *Lucifer* aired for the first time. This show is a perfect example of satan at work using two of his best weapons, **lying and deception.** The description of the show paints a fantasy type of satan. Pay close attention and you may see his cunning side come into focus.

Three men who wrote parts for characters in this show only included <u>one</u> true thing about satan: he is a "fallen angel." For everything else in the description, it seems they collaborated with satan himself about what to write. Lucifer was satan's name <u>before</u> he was kicked out of heaven; afterwards his name became satan, also known as the devil. They are not even using his "real" name.

They write that satan "has become dissatisfied with his life in hell..." Actually, satan is <u>not</u> in hell at this time. He circles and roams the earth freely tempting people to live in sin so he can separate them from God. We are warned in 1 Peter 5:8:

"Be sober, be vigilant; because your adversary the devil, as a roaring lion, walketh about, seeking whom he may devour."

In this context, <u>sober</u> means self-controlled and <u>vigilant</u> means to keep careful watch for possible danger. This warning is so important because God knows if we are "sober" and "vigilant" as He tells us to be, we can avoid an array of problems.

A day will come when satan, the one who deceives many, is thrown into the Lake of Fire and Brimstone for eternity (Revelation 20:10). When he is punished, he will be much more than "dissatisfied."

Next, they say satan "abandons his throne" and "retires to Los Angeles." This is false. Though his power is limited, it is the only power he has. He loves his throne and would never give it up. He is the commander of demons (Ephesians 6:12) and controls those outside of God's protection (Ephesians 2:1-3).

These three men talk about satan as if he is <u>just</u> a man looking for a second chance to live a life he previously had. He does not live like a man because he is <u>not</u>

a man. He has no interest in living in LA and has no obligation to stay in any particular place.

Then they mention satan's favorite things are "indulging in women, wine and music." **Indulge means** – allowing oneself to enjoy the pleasure of. He does indulge in women but not the way the show displays this. The show portrays satan as if he is a "ladies man." His role is quite different than that. He is the reason women are trapped in prostitution, sex trafficking and the porn industry, and knows this destroys men too.

This could be a long list but to sum it up, satan's goal in to destroy women and use them to destroy anyone else around them. "Destruction" is the only gift satan has for all women.

Yes he indulges in wine and all alcohol but not because he drinks it... He especially likes to get thrills from alcoholics, from people who drive drunk and kill others, and those who drink themselves to death. He also likes the ones who think that they can drink all of their problems away, men and women who stagger as they walk before passing out. He encourages them and whispers his favorite lies into their ears.

Last but not least, music. Yes, satan definitely indulges in music; he is very busy promoting promiscuous sexual relationships, drugs and alcohol to all artists, musicians and fans. He loves using music to influence a whole culture or even just a specific group of people. Let's take mainstream Hip Hop for example. This music teaches that women are sex objects and nothing more. Women learn they should only wear tight revealing clothes while dancing the most provocative way they can in music videos.

What does this music teach the men? You have to be a thug, have tattoos, get high, get drunk, be in a gang to get respect and have a gun to shoot and kill other men. It teaches men to glorify murder (unless a cop does it), sell drugs and sag your pants (even with a belt on) so you look suspicious not just to cops, but to most people.

Gangbangers used to sag because the weight of the guns they carried would pull their pants down. Today boys and men sag their pants because they think it is cool and makes them look tough. In reality, it looks like no one showed them the correct way to wear pants.

A little more? Sure, satan really likes how the men do not respect women, especially the ones who treat women like their favorite sport, scoring points. Some of these men have kids but they are not fathers to them. They can't be role models or husbands because money and their "homies" are more important than family. Many of them choose slavery, they get an orange jump suit, commissary and a jail cell.

Let's not forget the rappers. Phony is cool these days. There are redundant fake stories about toughness. It seems the use of profanity while talking about sex, money, violence and drugs brings credibility. For a chosen few, they are rewarded with fame, millions of fans and plenty of money.

A bunch of lies and nonsense somehow turns into music. So many people buy this music and it is played on the radio. These artists have albums that have sin, demons, death and destruction all throughout their songs. Many of them don't let their own kids listen to their music. **This music glorifies and worships satan.** These artists sell poison to the community and it literally kills people. Some kids look up to these artists and try to live out what they hear in the lyrics.

Here's how some of the album titles of today's secular hip-hop music **should** read:

Let's Fornicate $9.99, *Let's Sell Drugs and Smoke Marijuana* $9.99, *My Homies are More Important than My Family* $12.99. *I Sell Poison and take YOUR Money* $8.99. *Who needs a job? I hustle homie* $5.99.

Check out a few more: *I Shoot and Kill People Just Like Me* $9.99, *I'm a Coward Selling Lies* $5. *I Know I Have Kids But can Somebody Else Raise Them?* $14.99. *Yo, I sold out for satan, come join me* $9.99 and *I'm in Jail Again...* $8.99.

Some of the song names may be a little different but satan's handiwork is all over the hip-hop industry. This is just one genre. He sure does love music. He uses it well and devours many.

Music is a special gift but can be detrimental to us if we are not careful. Stop listening to the garbage satan is using to poison your mind and soul. There are so many amazing artists who make good music! This music is not played on the radio. Be sure to visit the **Bonus Features** section of this book to listen to some **real music.**

Let's move on to the description of the show where satan finds two new characteristics within himself, "compassion and sympathy." These are definitely <u>not</u> characteristics of satan; he does not possess them. The description also mentions that satan has an interest in a detective named Chloe because her character "appears to possess an inherent goodness."

The writer's say satan is attracted to this woman because he is accustomed to being around the "worst of humanity." So satan, the most immoral demonic being who hates God (who is perfect), is attracted to a female detective who has good morals? This does not make any sense. One thing is clear; this show is satan's pathetic attempt to re-create himself to this world.

Then to top it all off, the description says, "Lucifer starts to wonder if there is hope for his soul." If deception could take steroids, this is it. The devil **does not** "wonder if there is hope for his soul." He knows exactly what the future holds in store for him. God created him with perfection. To be evil and rebel against God was his choice.

This fictitious TV series shows that these writers **have no idea who satan is. Somehow, they decided to make a show about a counterfeit satan.** He is using these men to promote his agenda. If you are a believer, please pray for these men to be released from satan's grip and that they will come to know God's Truth.

Do not miss this. **There is no re-inventing satan.** He is not a man; he does not have a mother. He has no compassion or sympathy and he is <u>not</u> sorry for opposing God. Please remember as it was mentioned already; his main goal is "to steal, to kill and to destroy" (John 10:10).

Realize this: satan sells <u>sin</u> for a living. What have you bought? Give it back or get rid of it!

Sexual Perversion

Sexual sin is another area satan focuses on to <u>ruin</u> us. Fornication, rape, adultery and lust are some of his weapons. Sexual sin wrecks individuals, leaves relationships in devastation and destroys families. Have you noticed how much sex is promoted but not commitment or marriage?

Think about TV shows, movies, billboards, commercials, music, books and magazines, the internet and the media... It's everywhere; satan has caused confusion and created a dangerous weapon in perverting sex. God does not cause confusion (1 Corinthians 14:33), so we know this comes from satan.

In Leviticus 18:6-30, God shares in great detail about standards for us regarding sexual perversions that are inappropriate and forbidden so we can avoid them. Fornication, committing adultery, marrying relatives, having sexual relations with close relatives, homosexual relations and sexual relations with animals are **abominations and wicked to God.**

To those who have a spouse and family, would it be ok if one or all of your siblings had sexual relations with your spouse? What about your spouse having sexual relations with your mother or father? This would definitely cause some problems between you and your spouse, right?

At the very least, the two of you may need to have a "talk" and it wouldn't be a surprise if things went further than that... Out of hurt and anger, divorce may occur, violence may ensue, etc. People living during the days when the Old Testament was written and beforehand were doing these things just like we are today.

It is important to recognize that these things are not sinful and wrong because an opinionated person or some random individual thinks so, **but because God says so.** God punished the people living during the days of the Old Testament because of their disobedience.

The problems in our society today are <u>not</u> new problems, **they are old problems we have been warned not to repeat.** Sadly, our society continues this behavior and more and more effort is going into trying to make these things acceptable. **Believers speak out against sin because sin brings the wrath of God.**

In Genesis 19:1-29, Sodom and Gomorrah were cities filled with wicked people and homosexuality ran rampant. God destroyed these cities by raining fire and brimstone from heaven. <u>Every</u> person and <u>everything</u> in these cities was burned beyond recognition. Only a man named Lot and his family were spared. **God specifically calls homosexuality an abomination.**

Leviticus 18:22 says, *"You shall not lie with a male as one lies with a female; it is an abomination"* (NASB).

According to the Encarta Dictionary, the word **abomination** means –

1. Something horrible - An object of intense disapproval or dislike.

2. Something shameful – something that is immoral, disgusting or shameful.

Make no mistake, God is not accepting of homosexuality or any sin.

In this case, it was the people's stubbornness to turn away from <u>homosexuality</u> that caused the destruction of Sodom and Gomorrah. The world today is once again taking homosexuality and testing God as if to spit in His face and say, **"God will not do anything."**

Some people live in rebellion and disobey God because they do not fear God. Those who do not know God may not understand that He often gives us time to turn away from sin before He responds with punishment. When God gives us time, He expects for us to **repent** and turn back to Him.

Repent means - to change, to feel regret about sin and change your ways or habits.

If you do not fear God now, a day will come when you will. God <u>does</u> get tired of sin, rebellion and wickedness.

Today some people think rainbows are a sign or a symbol of acceptance for homosexuality. **It is not.** Some employers put a small rainbow on job applications. There are rainbow colored wristbands, sweatbands, shirts, organized events, etc. The cartoon "Care Bears" and the popular candy known as "Skittles" have nothing to do with rainbows either.

In the Bible, Genesis chapters 7 and 8 tell us about **the Great Flood.** God was so displeased with all the wicked, evil, corrupt and violent behavior during this time that He decided to flood the entire earth. It rained 40 days and 40 nights (Genesis 7:12) **"and everything was under water, even the highest mountain" (Genesis 7:19-20).** A man named Noah and his family were the only people God spared.

Genesis 9:8-17 tells us exactly why rainbows appear in the sky. Everyone should be extremely grateful that rainbows *do* appear. God made a specific covenant with man and every living creature (Genesis 9:15). The rainbow is a symbol and reminder of that covenant.

This is why it is so great to see a rainbow in the sky. It means God will never destroy the entire earth by water again to punish sin. The fact that a rainbow is amazing to look at is a bonus. No person, group of people, cartoon, candy or anything else in this world can change what the Rainbow represents. **God made the Rainbow.**

God *does* punish sin (2 Peter 2:4-9) **and He chooses when.** In James 4:2-4 we are warned about the consequences of sin. If you have struggled with your sexual orientation, maybe the thought, "I was born this way" has crept into your mind. **This is a lie from satan.** From now on, you have a choice. **You can accept this lie or reject this lie.** You do <u>not</u> have to accept this but know that satan wants you to.

Scientific studies support that people who have experienced anxiety, abuse, neglect, mental health disorders and other problems struggle with their sexual orientation. 31 years ago, homosexuality was listed in *The Diagnostic and Statistical Manual of Mental Disorders* (DSM). In the 1980's, this was psychiatry's standard reference on classifying mental illness. So **sin** was called something else, "mental illness".

Please understand this: People don't decide what "sin" is, God decides.

Now look where we are today, ignoring God and making new laws. This is how **sin** spreads and grows. God gave us laws, order and boundaries for a reason. Who decided to make new laws that defy God? Now **sin** is demanding rights, it has protests and wants to be treated equal. Now it is legal for sin to get married and sue anyone who stands in its way. It seems **sin** can become a person or a group of people. It can be disguised many ways. **Sexual sin** is one of satan's favorite weapons.

Homosexuality is **not** an issue that starts before or during birth but after. Satan can control and manipulate those on his team (See Ephesians 2:1-4). A non-believer will fight against and oppose the ways of God. Here's the bottom line, anyone living a homosexual lifestyle must realize two things:

1. You have been deceived by satan or he is currently trying to deceive you. Living this lifestyle is a choice <u>you</u> make. You openly defy God. You obey satan and live the way he wants you to live. This is a scary place to be. If you're not worried, you <u>should</u> be.

2. Now is the time for you to make another choice. Jesus is the only One who can bring change to your situation. **No matter who you are, if you're looking for a way out, Jesus is the way.** He is able to do more than you could ever think or imagine. Make a decision. Will you fully depend on Jesus and get the

life He has for you? Or will you let satan take your life and rule it?

Know this; God did <u>not</u> make a mistake in anything He created.

Psalms 139:13-14 says, *"For You formed my innermost parts; You knit me [together] in my mother's womb. I will give thanks and praise to You, for I am fearfully and wonderfully made"* (NASB).

God knows who He created each individual person to be. Yes, this includes you. But we have to follow Him and let Him shows us. We <u>cannot</u> run from God, there is no place we can go to get away from Him. **Make a huge decision, stop living in disobedience and start obeying God.**

If you are living a homosexual lifestyle or are dealing with any kind of sexual sin (pornography, fornication, adultery, etc.) you are <u>not</u> doomed. Thinking that way is the way satan wants you to think. **It is not too late, but you must take immediate action.**

You <u>can</u> choose to stop living a sinful lifestyle. Sin is the result of rebellion. Stop rebelling. Do not live in isolation. For additional help or resources please see the contact information in the *"Wait, how can I switch teams"* section.

Your will to fight is what satan wants to take from you. Do not let him; you have to be willing to fight back.

Genesis 1:27 says, *"So God created man in His own image, in the image of God created He them; male and female created He them."*

God created us in His own image! God is spirit; this means every person is spirit. God formed our bodies from the dirt. Therefore, your spirit was put into a dirt body. You are special and uniquely made. Your body has its own fingerprint, no two finger prints are the same! There are so many cool things about the human body. But, the point here is that you are responsible for controlling your body.

Our spirit and body can only function at its best when we live God's way. He gave us the Bible to help us (more on this later). In short, the Bible is like God's playbook for us. It contains all God's instructions for us to live the best life possible and defeat our opponent which is satan. Jeremiah 29:11 says,

"For I know the plans that I have for you,' declares the LORD, 'plans for welfare and not for calamity to give you a future and a hope." (NASB).

However, satan has a playbook of his own. His playbook contains rebellion against God's ways. It has some bad cleverly disguised as good, many lies, distractions and ways to keep you away from God and is full of evil. His playbook is full of garbage. Following satan's ways will ruin your spirit and body. Ultimately, it will lead you to live the worst life possible ending in destruction and Eternal Death.

Check this out. God gives you a car. The car comes with everything it needs to function, including an owner's manual. You are responsible for reading and knowing what is in the owner's manual. Why? Because it will help you know how to take care of the car.

If any warning lights come on the dashboard you will notice them and know what they mean. You will know what you need to do and can handle the problem. You will be able to maintain the car. You control the car. You decide if you want to drive it through a car wash to make it clean. You control how fast it goes, whether it goes straight or turns, which lane it drives in and how to get where you're going.

In this illustration, <u>you</u> are the spirit, <u>you</u> are responsible for the car. The car is the body. The owner's manual is the Bible. Get the picture? Now, do you control your body or does your body control you?

The intricate anatomy of the male and female body is at the very least amazing. **It is more than obvious that only a man and a woman are to be husband and wife.** And to make sure this is clear, God gave us specific instructions about sexual relations.

Have you ever thought about how unique Adam and Eve were? They are the only two humans that never had an earthly mother or father. They did not have navels, never learned to crawl or walk and had no childhood. God created them as adults and they knew everything they needed to know. That is amazing!

God made Eve for Adam (Genesis 2:21-23). God instituted marriage. It was a gift for Adam and Eve and is *still* a gift today. God has standards. He knows what is best for us and expects us to follow in His ways.

For a man and a woman who are <u>not</u> married, it is the man's responsibility to lead and to honor God in that relationship. This means communicating expectations and setting boundaries as necessary is the man's responsibility. God expects men to be responsible with what He gives to them.

Marriage is only acceptable to God in the way He created us: male and female, husband and wife.

Adam, the male and husband, and Eve, the female and wife. They were the very first marriage! It does not matter what the world or culture is doing today. Marriage was not created by culture; it is not for convenience and is not to be taken lightly. That being said, God created sex as a gift for marriage. This was not a mistake on His part. **There is no good reason to rebel against God's ways, only excuses.**

What happens when we follow satan's way and disregard God's way concerning sex?
Sexually Transmitted Diseases spread and kill people from generation to generation. Men and women are raped and many times die as a result. Men and women do not respect or love each other. Boys and girls are molested and sexually abused. They are sold as sex slaves and used for sex trafficking.

There is prostitution and pornography. Husbands and wives commit adultery. Fornication is acceptable as long as you have an excuse. The number of single parent homes drastically increases. Unmarried couples cheat on each other because they're <u>not</u> married and they don't feel there is a serious commitment. Some people do not care about being good parents or about parenting at all.

Babies are murdered **before** they're born. God hates abortion because it is murder and murder is sin. In Jeremiah 1:5 God tells us, *"Before I formed you in the womb I knew you"* (NASB). **It's scary that over 60 million babies in the United States have been murdered since 1973.** Does anyone care that murder in this way is legal?

This is what happens when we disobey God. God knows us before we are born. **He made sex a gift for marriage for a reason.** Satan loves abortion because his goal is to steal our lives. Over 60 million and counting, satan is stealing lives everyday. People are left in ruin and some cannot figure out why.

Following satan's ways leads men and women to burn with lust, creating as many broken homes as possible. Children suffer because they are the result of selfish desires. **Men and women as well as young boys and**

girls think sex = love. Some parents find it difficult to address sex with their kids because they had sex when they were just kids themselves.

Some boys and girls have sex at a young age because they think they "love" someone. What they think is love is actually lust. **Love is *not* similar to lust in any way.**

Lust means – uncontrolled or illicit sexual desire or appetite; lecherousness (Dictionary.com). All of this happens because of rebellion. We can learn about love from reading 1 Corinthians 13:4-7, which says:

"Love is patient, love is kind and is not jealous; love does not brag and is not arrogant, does not act unbecomingly; it does not seek its own, is not provoked, does not take into account a wrong suffered, does not rejoice in unrighteousness, but rejoices with truth; bears all things, believes all things, hopes all things, endures all things" (NASB).

This is how God wants all people to love each other. The enormous gap between lust and love is quite clear. Do you love anyone in your life like this? **Start really loving others like this.**

You already know what the world's love is like: fake, phony, manipulative, impatient, careless, arrogant, selfish, vengeful, inconsistent, unreliable, full of lies, cheating, secret agendas and motives. This is **not** love.

The bottom line is that God has <u>not</u> changed love or His standards for marriage.

Are you in a relationship that clearly goes against God's standards? *If so, this is a wakeup call for you.* Are you unmarried but living together as if you *are* married? Stop using the "Everyone else is doing it" excuse or this one, "Well, we are saving on rent."

Men, step up to the plate and take the initiative. Move out and get your own place. Some couples may stay together and some may not. **If you value your relationship, do it the right way. God's way is better than your way.** Focus on being the person God created you to be so your marriage can be the special and sacred gift God created it to be. This process may take some time but its well worth it. Ladies, this requires you to do your part as well.

Take a moment to ask yourself this question, "Do I genuinely care about living the way God wants me to live?"

Living God's way is the best way you could ever live. His standards, rules and laws have a purpose.

Can you imagine living in a world with no laws and no consequences? What would driving be like without any lines, medians, guardrails or speed limits? Driving would be a nightmare, it's already dangerous now! Who would stop criminals if there were no Law Enforcement? What if there was no right or wrong? What if there was only hate and/or evil and no love?

What if there were no referees to enforce the rules in sports? What would football be without penalties and touchdowns, tennis without lines and a net, soccer without goals, basketball without fouls and rims?

What if there was no such thing as rape? What if men could choose to have sex with any woman or women could choose to have sex with any man? There are places in the world where people already live this way.

The list could go on but one thing is certain, this world would be much worse than it is already. There would be more evil and more violence. Without God, there would be no right or wrong. No beautiful green grass, trees or sunrises and sunsets. No love or anything good at all.

Where are the men who will step up? When men follow God's ways and lead, men win. Their families win, society wins, everyone benefits. Where are the women who will step up? When women follow God's ways, men can be at their best. Families can flourish and communities can thrive. **God has expectations for men and women. It is time to start meeting those expectations.**

There are 3 basic aspects for Marriage. **First**, the man promises himself to his wife in a public ceremony. **Second**, the man and woman promise to love each other above all others and they are joined together by taking responsibility for each other's welfare. **Third**, the husband and wife become "one" in the commitment and intimacy of sexual union (Genesis 2:24-25).

Strong marriages have a foundation of: commitment to each other, deep companionship, real oneness and the absence of shame. Divorce was never in God's plan for marriage, that came from us. There are consequences for replacing God's love with satan's lies.

How many more marriages would be the special relationship God designed them to be if we followed His standards?

Take notice, God did not create Adam and Steve (two males) or Eve and Adamiesha (two females) for each other. **God made this so clear and simple yet men and women <u>choose</u> to act in rebellion.** Sex has been perverted to a sickening level: adultery, fornication, rape, pornography, sex between close relatives or family members, homosexuality, sex between people and animals. People are even marrying animals.

We have all these things happening in our world today. Punishment will come in these days for the same reason it came to generations before, because people refuse to repent, turn away from sin and continue to rebel against and disobey God.

What can satan and his team look forward to?

Satan laughs when the consequences of sin unfold. Make no mistake, satan is serious about his business, he hates everyone and rejoices only in the destruction of people. His end game is **Eternal Death** and his goal is that **You** are eternally separated from God as he will be.

He will do anything and everything in his power to oppose God; this includes getting as many people as possible to join him. Remember, satan is against everyone, even those who are on his team. But his destiny is sealed: eternity in the **Lake of Fire and Brimstone** where he will be "tormented day and night forever and ever." (Revelation 20:10).

Truth: No one has to stay a non-believer.

All non-believers are members of satan's team and will join him "in the lake that burns with fire and brimstone" (Revelation 21:8). Everyone in this place will experience agony, suffering, torment, torture and misery for <u>Eternity</u>. In this world, many people don't seem too concerned about this. Think about it and if possible, see if you can comprehend just a little bit of what this place will be like. The next two paragraphs may help a little bit.

Your future is now very predictable; there will be no surprises in Eternal Death. Your new home, The Lake of Fire and Brimstone, is permanent. You will never own material things to move to a new place or encounter new surroundings again. You will have a new eternal body and will never die again. Everyone here will be tormented day and night, forever along with satan and demons. What if you get hungry, thirsty or need to take a break from torment?

You will not eat. There will not be any seafood, no meat of any kind, no vegetarian, vegan or gluten-free diets, no candy and no dessert. There will be no need to be concerned about GMO's in your food. You will not drink. No water, coffee, beer or alcohol, soda or favorite protein shake: nothing to quench your thirst.

No sleep, no rest, no bed or pillow, no relaxing, no watching your favorite TV show or movies, no Wi-Fi, no cell phone. No social media or going to "the club." No hanging out and chilling with your friends.

No smoking marijuana, cigars, cigarettes, e-cigarettes or anything else. No drugs of any kind. No Tylenol, Advil or morphine to lessen the agony that will never go away. There will not be any breaks. No one will be able to call a timeout. There will **NEVER** be any kind of relief. Your <u>best</u> days will be the life you lived before you died. **At this moment, it will be clear to you that your past life lead you here but it will be too late to change it.**

The worst part is not the torment, the suffering, gnashing of teeth, the screams or even the fire. It's being separated from God forever. The complete absence of God's presence. Nothing anyone has ever experienced on Earth will compare to this place.

Because God created Heaven, it will be <u>more</u> awesome than anyone could ever imagine. But because God created The Lake of Fire and Brimstone, it will be <u>more</u> horrific than anyone could ever imagine.

There is only one who tries to keep this hidden from us. It is satan. He loves for people to think they are "living life to the fullest" until it is <u>too</u> late.

What does "too late" mean?

Well here is the answer: if you have lived your life in rebellion against God and suddenly breathed your last breath... too late. Then satan has great joy in knowing that he gets to say, "gotcha." **Eternal Death** is really the best that satan has to offer anyone on his team AND check this out, it's free...

Now ask yourself this question:

Am I <u>choosing</u> to share in satan's punishment by the way I am currently living?

Jesus's Team - Eternal Life

The roster for the **Winning team** includes The One and only True God who exists in three persons. **God the Father, God the Son (Jesus) and God the Holy Spirit, Angels in heaven and all Believers.**

God is the Creator of all; He is holy, all-powerful, all knowing, good and perfect. God is spirit; He is not limited by time, space or matter. He is infinite and everlasting. God is truthful, loving and just. He judges sin. He offers grace, mercy and forgiveness. **God made a way to redeem all people from the curse of sin and death in sending Jesus.**

We cannot fully comprehend God; His ways are not our ways. However, just to be clear, His ways are much better than our ways. God desires for every person to have **Eternal Life**. Eternal Life means - Eternity with God in Heaven. This is just a brief introduction, there could never be enough to say about God.

Jesus is the reason no one has to stay on satan's team. Because of Jesus, we can switch teams. We can have **Eternal Life**. Jesus' invitation to join His team is open to every individual person. **Salvation** is possible and offered to us freely as a gift **only** because of Jesus (more on this later). "Salvation" means we are delivered from God's wrath and the consequences of sin, which is <u>Eternal Death</u>.

Truth: The gift of Salvation is offered to Every person freely and is either accepted or rejected by each individual person.

Jesus **promises** salvation and eternal life to those who believe in Him (John 14:1-3). Jesus provides a way for us to escape the penalty of sin, restore our relationship with God and receive Eternal Life. You must have a relationship with Jesus to know Him. How do you develop a relationship with someone? You have to spend time with them and get to know them. Can you honestly say you *know* Jesus?

Timeout: make time in your life to know Jesus.

Without Jesus, there is no one to intercede on our behalf.

No one is like Jesus, no person who has ever lived compares to Jesus, period.

Sometimes you may hear or read "Jesus Christ." **Christ** means Chosen One, Anointed One or Messiah. This means Jesus was sent from God to deliver us from sin and Eternal Death. "Christ" is His title, not His last name.

God sends the **Holy Spirit** to indwell in believers (1 Corinthians 6:19-20). The Holy Spirit is the "seal" of salvation for those who believe in Jesus (Ephesians 1:13-14). He, the Holy Spirit, regenerates and renews believers (Titus 3:5), **fights against the "flesh"** (Galatians 5:16-18) and produces the fruit of the spirit in believers (Galatians 5:22-25).

The Holy Spirit works among non-believers to lead them to Jesus. He convicts people's hearts of sin, provides them with an understanding of righteousness and shows them a way out of judgment (John 16:8). The Holy Spirit provides wisdom to believers to understand the teaching of God revealed in Scripture (1 Corinthians 2:10-13). A person cannot accept truth from the Holy Spirit if they reject God. This is just some of what the Holy Spirit does.

Angels are special beings created by God. Have you ever seen a picture of a baby with wings? **Spoiler alert:** there are no angel babies. Angels are <u>not</u> human beings and people do <u>not</u> turn into angels. In short, they are God's holy servants and are obedient to His commands.

A **Believer** is a child of God born again by faith (John 3:3), believing and trusting in the work of Jesus Christ. A believer acknowledges sin, asks Jesus to forgive all their sins, believes that Jesus (who never sinned) shed His blood on the cross and died to pay for their sins and the sins of the world. Believers believe that Jesus rose from the dead three days after His death, defeating the power of sin and death (death meaning eternal separation from God).

A believer is willing to turn away from sin, invites Jesus into their heart to have a personal relationship with Him and fully accepts **salvation** through faith in Jesus Christ.

Believers are often called Christians. The word "Christian" literally means, "belonging to the party of Christ" or "follower of Christ." Believers/Christians are members of Jesus's team and will spend eternity with God and Angels in heaven.

God loves us

God's amazing love for us is impossible to fully comprehend. John 3:16-17 says:

"For God so loved the world, that He gave His only begotten Son, that whoever believes in Him shall not perish, but have eternal life. For God did not send the Son into the world to judge the world, but that the world might be saved through Him." (NASB)

God came down from Heaven in the person of Jesus, the Son of God to destroy the works of the devil (1 John 3:8). God chose Joseph and Mary (who were engaged), to be the parents of Jesus. God sent the angel Gabriel to Mary to explain that she would give birth to a Son and that she was to name Him Jesus (Luke 1:26-38). Mary was a virgin when she conceived Jesus. **This was a work of the Holy Spirit.**

Joseph did not believe Mary and was going to divorce her quietly. Because sex is for marriage (after the wedding), this was a big deal. Put yourself in Joseph's shoes. Your fiancée tells you that she is pregnant, the name chosen for your child without your input and that she did <u>not</u> cheat on you. Honestly, would you have believed Mary?

Nevertheless, Joseph would come to know the truth. The angel of the Lord appeared to Joseph in a dream confirming what Mary told him about the birth of Jesus that would take place. Joseph was instructed to move forward with the wedding so he did (Matthew 1:18-25).

The sinful nature of all human beings is passed down through Adam because we are his descendants. Sin has been passed down through every man since Adam. **Jesus is the only exception**. Because Mary was a virgin and conceived Jesus by the Holy Spirit, He was uniquely born <u>without</u> a sinful nature. This is why Jesus could <u>not</u> have a human biological father.

Who else has been born this way?
No one, Only Jesus.

Jesus was born in Israel during the days of King Herod. This king ordered all boys 2 years old and younger to be killed in the area where Jesus was. His plan was to kill Jesus. In Matthew 2:13, we learn the angel of the Lord appeared to Joseph in another dream, telling him to take Mary and Jesus to Egypt. Joseph, Mary and Jesus returned to Israel after King Herod died (Matthew 2:19-21).

Jesus was God in the flesh; God was literally among us in a human body. He was both fully human and fully divine at the same time. John 1:14 says:

"And the Word became flesh, and dwelt among us, and we saw His glory, glory as of the only begotten from the Father, full of grace and truth."

Before Jesus was born as a baby, He was in heaven. John 1:1-3 reads, *"In the beginning was the Word, and the Word was with God, and the Word was God. ² He was in the beginning with God.³ All things came into being through Him, and apart from Him nothing came into being that has come into being."* (NASB).

Jesus makes it clear that He is God. In John 10:30 He says, *"I and my Father are one."* This is the clearest statement Jesus ever made regarding His divinity.

God the Father, God the Son (Jesus) and God the Holy Spirit are <u>not</u> the same person (Matthew 3:16-17), but they are one in essence and in nature. So no, <u>not</u> 1+1+1=3 but rather 1x1x1=1, that's right, one God. If this is hard to understand, be encouraged. Our minds do

JESUS vs satan · 69

not understand everything about God. After all He created us, not the other way around.

God tells us not to lie, steal or commit murder. These things are wrong. Doing these things would mean we are rebelling against God. Rebellion results in sin. **God loves people but *hates* all sin.** There is no such thing as a small sin or big sin to God. Lying is no better than murder: sin is sin, period. Sin has consequences and must be paid for. Think of something important that you have purchased. Unless you stole that item, you paid for it with cash, a credit/debit card, money order, apple pay, PayPal, etc. However, these forms of payment cannot pay for sins…

For our sins to be forgiven a sacrifice must be made and blood must be shed. Before Jesus came, animals were offered as sacrifices for sins (Leviticus 4:32-35). A priest was appointed to perform the sacrifice for each individual in the community. Every time someone committed a sin, a priest had to perform a sacrifice for them.

With just a little effort, you can imagine how this happened repeatedly. Can you imagine having to do that today? What animal would you need to get and where would you get it? Where would you need to take the animal and who would perform the steps required to complete the sacrifice for you? This would be quite a task today but because of Jesus, no one has to go through this process.

Truth: Because Jesus was <u>not</u> born with a sinful nature, only Jesus could be the perfect sacrifice for the sins of the entire world.

Jesus has the power and authority to forgive sins (Matthew 9:1-8). **Jesus came and paid the cost of <u>all</u> sin** (Hebrews 9:11-28). This means He paid for the sins of <u>every</u> single person in the world. Right now there are more than 7.5 billion people in the world. We'll just round it off at 7.5 billion. If you need a visual of this, go to this website and scroll down for a couple minutes: http://www.7billionworld.com.

Let's say each individual person sinned 10 times per week for a 1 year, Monday thru Friday <u>only</u>. That means each of us would commit 2 sins a day. **In 1 year that would equal 3.9 trillion sins.** Jesus paid for **ALL** of those sins. He paid for so much more because He paid for **ALL** the sins of <u>every</u> person in the world.

How much would it cost you to pay for just one sin? You would have to spend eternity in the Lake of Fire to pay for <u>one</u> sin. This is a **Life sentence**, no parol, no early release because you realize that Jesus is real and you made a mistake. This would be the biggest mistake you ever made and being sorry won't change anything.

Have you committed even one sin in your lifetime? The answer to this question for <u>every</u> single person in the world is a resounding "Yes."

There are only two acceptable payments for sin.

1. You pay - This means you are a **non-believer**, a member of satan's team. You have chosen to live in rebellion towards Jesus; you **reject** Him and do not believe in Him. You reject the <u>free</u> gift of Salvation that only Jesus offers and decline His offer to pay for you. By now, it is clear that you have decided to pay for yourself. Your payment will be declined because you do not have the power to remove your own sins. You have a personal debt to address.

There is a price for sin and it <u>will</u> be paid.

No one can pay using cash, a money order, a check or electronically. It is important to point out that satan **cannot** remove sin. This means satan **does not pay** the cost of sin for anyone on his team.

Therefore, <u>without</u> Jesus, Your sins <u>still</u> exist.

You + satan = Eternal Death (Lake of Fire).

2. Jesus Pays – This means you are a **believer**, a member of Jesus' team! You have **accepted** the <u>free</u> gift of Salvation that only Jesus offers. You believe in Him, know Him and love Him. You have asked Jesus to be your personal Savior! Your life has been transformed by Jesus and this transformation is ongoing. You do not live the same way you lived as a non-believer.

You realize that Jesus paid a price for you that no one else could pay. **Only Jesus can remove sin.** You are <u>with</u> Jesus; you will experience victory over sin and over satan.

You accept that Jesus paid the price for your sin.

You + Jesus = Eternal Life (Heaven).

Has anyone ever told you, "Jesus Loves You or God Loves You?" If so, this person is trying to let you know, you do not have to accept satan's offer. You do not have to pay.

Wake up! Jesus paid for you! He took God's wrath that was meant for you upon Himself. He wants you in Heaven with Him. Jesus wants to have a personal relationship with you! This is huge, this is personal. Jesus wants a personal relationship with <u>every</u> individual person.

A time will come when Jesus will stop offering to pay. <u>Grace</u> and <u>Mercy</u> will not last always. A time will come when there will only be one form of payment: You pay.

Jesus paid for more than we can ever fully understand. Every individual person <u>could</u> be forgiven of their sins. Every person <u>could</u> be who God created them to be and go to Heaven. **God does not want any person to suffer as satan and demons will in the Lake of Fire.**

Each individual person can go to Jesus directly; **He is the only one who can wipe our slate clean.** Unfortunately, many non-believers will stay on satan's team and will not acknowledge or accept what Jesus has done for them. Non-believers refuse to repent, ask for forgiveness and believe in Jesus for their salvation. They choose the "You pay" option.

This is a warning to anyone reading this book:
This is Your choice.

What exactly did Jesus do for me?

Jesus did not have a physical body until He came to earth. **Jesus came down from Heaven to save us.** Take a minute to think about that. He left Heaven and put on flesh to do what no one else could do. He did so willingly because He loves us.

Imagine that you live in a huge mansion and own everything you ever wanted. Maybe you are reading this and you already do. Would you leave your house and everything you own to be homeless and live in a homeless community instead? Let's be honest, probably not. Even if you did, it would not compare to Jesus leaving Heaven to come to this world.

Jesus suffered for our sake, taking the punishment we deserve. "Our sake" means every single person in the world. He was truly innocent but was hated by the religious leaders of His day. They held an illegal trial and sentenced Jesus to death by crucifixion. This is how criminals were put to death and was the worst way anyone could die.

Jesus speaks of the hatred the world has towards Him and the hatred the world has towards believers (John 15:18-27). He was found guilty without cause but this was God's plan. Jesus gave Himself for us willingly.

Before the Crucifixion, Jesus was scourged. Scourging itself can cause death. During this time, the Romans used a flag rum whip, which consisted of pieces of bone and metal attached to multiple leather strands. His skin was ripped off His body. The first strikes would tear through the skin and through fat tissue.

Next, this whip would start tearing through muscles, tendons and all the blood vessels supplying these areas. This resulted in extreme blood loss and exposed tissue and bones. The person who performed this form of torture enjoyed doing this. Jesus was then forced to carry His own crossbar, typically weighing 100-110 pounds, to the place where He was crucified.

In addition, He suffered a severe beating from Roman soldiers. They punched Jesus, spit on Him and forced a crown of thorns down on His head. The type of thorns used at this time would have been one and a half to two inches long. This means Jesus would have had dozens of piercings in his scalp creating a significant amount of blood loss from His head. A person can bleed to death from just one scalp injury.

They also stripped Jesus' clothes, leaving Him naked. Take a minute to think of the horrible shame of this alone. Who else do you know that would do this for you willingly? That's right, no one. If you have kids, would you sacrifice one of them to die for a murderer, rapist or thief? Short answer, no. Can you see that Jesus did what no one else could? A love that no one else can copy.

Next, they nailed His hands and feet to the Cross. Hanging on a cross in this position causes suffocation. Jesus had to go through agonizing pain for each breath; this could only be done by using his legs to push upwards.

While hanging, His side was pierced with a spear. Many people were watching this as it was happening. **Why did Jesus come down from heaven to be**

treated this way? Jesus chose to die this way because this is what He had to do in order to pay for the sins of every single person in the world.

What do you think about Jesus going through <u>all</u> of this just for you?

Truth: Let's make this perfectly clear. Jesus did <u>not</u> die for your sins because you deserved it. No one in this world deserves what Jesus endured on the cross. He did it because He loves us.

Historical records are very clear; Jesus suffered hours of terrible sustained torture both before and on the cross. Many credible scientists and scholars (even non-believers) attest to the four Gospels in the Bible being accurate in their historical accounts of Jesus. **The Crucifixion of Jesus is undeniable**. The four Gospels are found in the New Testament in the Bible: Matthew, Mark, Luke and John. These are personal life accounts from these four men who lived with Jesus and witnessed His Crucifixion.

Yes, Jesus is in fact a historical figure but He is much more than that. <u>Three</u> days after His death,

Jesus rose from the dead defeating the power of sin and death.

Following Jesus' Resurrection, He appeared to two believers who were traveling, walking and talking with them (Luke 24:13-33). He also appeared to His disciples and others before ascending into Heaven (see Luke 24).

Jesus never sinned. He allowed Himself to be "made sin" to save us (2 Corinthians 5:21), bearing the world's sin to make us acceptable to God. **It is this act of love that makes it possible for us to receive salvation and be saved.** Ephesians 2:8 says, *"For by grace are ye saved through faith; and that not of yourselves: it is the gift of God."* It is truly a gift, a very special gift <u>anyone</u> can receive.

How long would it take you to receive a free new car, SUV or truck? You would ask, "Where do I sign?!"

Would you receive 1 million dollars if someone offered to give it to you? After making sure there were no strings attached, sure! Yes, this would be great.

However, a vehicle can be stolen, wrecked or destroyed by a tornado, hailstorm or flooding. Money can be stolen, spent, lost, etc. People are killed for money.

The point is, these are material things that can be taken away at any time.

Jesus offers Salvation and it cannot be stolen! **Jesus** is the only way to Eternal Life. **Without Jesus there is no Salvation.** Acts 4:12 says:

"And there is salvation in no one else; for there is no other name under heaven that has been given among men by which we must be saved." (NASB).

Salvation comes only through Jesus. His name brings healing, hope, joy and peace. There is power in the name of **Jesus**! Now you know the **Gospel**, which means, the Good News. It is The Incarnation, Life, Birth, Death, Burial, The Resurrection and the expected return of Jesus. **There is no one like Jesus!** He saw joy in defeating satan, sin and eternal death, choosing to suffer more than we could ever understand so we could be saved. Hebrews 12:2 says,

"Fixing our eyes on Jesus, the author and perfecter of faith, who for the joy set before Him endured the cross, despising the shame, and has sat down at the right hand of the throne of God."

Timeout
Jesus commands us to follow Him.

There is no other Faith in the world where the Life of the Founder is the foundation of the Faith. Jesus is the foundation!

No one compares to Jesus, not even close.

Jesus is in a class all by Himself. Jesus is in a league of His own. Faith in Jesus Christ is unmatched.

Religion cannot forgive sins, only Jesus can.

Now let's briefly talk about the hate and disrespect people have towards **Jesus**, even after all He has done for everyone. In movies, actors use the name **Jesus** like a profane word. This also happens in normal conversation as if nothing is wrong with it. In Exodus 20:7 God specifically addresses this. This verse reads:

"You shall not take the name of the LORD your God in vain, for the LORD will not leave him unpunished who takes His name in vain."

What if God suddenly decided to punish everyone who has said the name **Jesus** in a profane way? A great number (impossible to estimate) of people in this world would be punished.

If you are reading this and you have ever said God or the name Jesus in a profane manner, repent right now and do not let it happen again.

Why don't people use satan's name in a profane way? He's the enemy. Why not curse the names of all the false gods? After all Jesus has done for us, people reject Him and curse His name. Are you one of them?

God's mercy and patience with us goes beyond our understanding but make no mistake, this mercy and patience can come to an end. Are you testing God by the words you choose to use and the way you live?

Worldly things cannot compare to what Jesus has to offer. **Be careful if you think you have time.** If you **have not** received Salvation through Jesus, how much time have you wasted already? If you're reading this, God has given you time. How many seconds, minutes, hours, days, weeks, months and years has God given you?

You are alive and breathing right now only because God has given you life. Yes, God gives us life and He knows the exact amount of time we have. However, we don't know how much time we have. Think about that. Don't waste the time God gives you.

Simply put, **we cannot earn salvation.** We cannot change this based on how many good deeds we do or by being a **"good person."** Romans 3:23 says, "For all have sinned and come short of the glory of God." This scripture says "All" which means every individual person.

The sin payment test

In case you are pondering this, you can ask yourself the following questions (the answers are already provided):

Can I forgive my own sins? **Answer:** No.

If I die, can I raise myself from the dead by my own power? **Answer:** No.

I've done so many bad things, I have so much guilt and shame inside of me, is it possible that Jesus would love and forgive someone like me? **Answer:** Yes, Jesus does love you and will forgive you if you sincerely ask Him. He loves you more than you could ever understand.

Who did God raise from the dead and who has power to forgive my sins? **Answer:** Only Jesus!

Who is like Jesus? **Answer:** No one.

Who else has done what Jesus has done for you? **Answer:** No one.

God is Love. Love would not exist without God. God first loved us (1 John 4:19) and sent Jesus to shed His blood on the cross to save and free us from sin. Anyone who <u>chooses</u> to remain in sin has chosen satan's team and will suffer the consequences of sin.

What does Jesus look like?

Now let's briefly address a question many people wonder about. What did/does Jesus look like? Let's look at the scriptures. Isaiah 53:2 tells us,

"He hath no form nor comeliness; and when we shall see him, there is no beauty that we should desire him."

This refers to when Jesus came 2,000 years ago and it was prophesied in Isaiah 53:1-2, which was written between 701-681 BC. This prophecy was fulfilled around 31 AD, so over 700 years before Jesus came!

Have you ever seen someone portraying Jesus in a play or in a movie? If so, you probably would not describe Jesus like that right? Could you land the lead playing role and be the lead actor with a description like that? This certainly does not sound like the description of someone who would be chosen to play the leading role...

Referring to when Jesus returns to earth from Heaven, John shares a vision of Jesus in Revelation 1:14-15:

"His head and His hairs were white like wool, as white as snow; and his eyes were as a flame of fire; and

His feet like unto fine brass, as if they were burned in a furnace; and His voice as the sound of many waters."

What a powerful vision! Now this is referring to Jesus' new resurrected and glorified body. Nevertheless, these are the two distinct descriptions of Jesus in the Bible. Obviously, man has created a false portrayal of Jesus. People who lived in this region of the world during this time were certainly not white or European in appearance, as Jesus is shown in many pictures and movies.

There are no drawings or portraits of Jesus in the Bible. Who decided a portrait of Jesus should be made in the first place? The only people who know what Jesus looked like were the people who saw Him when He was here.

However, knowing exactly what Jesus looks like is not what is most important. What matters most is <u>who</u> He is, <u>what</u> He did and whether you <u>know</u> Him or not. Maybe not a satisfying answer for some. But a time will come when everyone will see Jesus! When He returns there will be no confusion. Philippians 2:10-11 reads:

"so that all created beings in heaven and on earth—even those long ago dead and buried—will bow

in worship before this Jesus Christ, and call out in praise that he is the Master of all, to the glorious honor of God the Father." (The Message).

Revelation 1:7 says, "Riding the clouds, he'll be seen by every eye, those who mocked and killed him will see him, People from all nations and all times will tear their clothes in lament. Oh, Yes." (The Message). Only Jesus will crack open the sky and ride through on clouds! When Jesus returns, All people will see Him and know it is Him without question.

Is Jesus really for Everyone?

Jesus transcends culture and religion. He wants to have a personal relationship with each one of us and free us from sin to be men and women who bring Glory to God. **Jesus shows us the importance of "Relationship."** As people, we often see only the outside of others but Jesus always sees inside (1 Samuel 16:7). He is most concerned about our heart. No matter what race or ethnic group a person is, **Jesus is for everyone**, not just a select few (Romans 10:9-13).

Do not let satan deceive you into believing this: "Well I'm from (fill in the blank), this is my culture and what we believe and that's just the way it is…" **EVERY person in the world is a member of either Jesus' team or satan's team.** There are <u>No exceptions</u>!

The only way to God is through Jesus.

In John 14:6, Jesus says, *"I am the way, and the truth, and the life; no one comes to the Father but through Me" (NASB).*

Anyone who does not believe in Jesus is on satan's team (John 3:16-20). It is **impossible** for anyone to hold a neutral stance or claim they don't belong to either team, for in Matthew 12:30 Jesus says:

"He who is not with me is against me; and he who does not gather with me scatters" (NASB).

Every person in the world is included in this one passage. See where you stand with this. John 3:19-21 tells us:

"This is the crisis we're in: God-light streamed into the world, but men and women everywhere ran for

the darkness. They went for the darkness because they were not really interested in pleasing God. Everyone who makes a practice of doing evil, addicted to denial and illusion, hates God-light and won't come near it, fearing a painful exposure. But anyone working and living in truth and reality welcomes God-light so the work can be seen for the God-work it is. "(The Message).

Jesus is the God-light, the Light of the world. John 1:4-5 says, *⁴ In Him was life, and the life was the Light of men.⁵ The Light shines in the darkness, and the darkness did not comprehend it. "* (NASB).

Why is The Bible so important?

The Bible is not just credible, it is infallible. 2 Timothy 3:16 tells us, *"All scripture is given by inspiration of God."* About 40 different authors contributed to the Bible. God used these men, with their individual and unique personalities, to write exactly what He told them to write, **resulting in the perfect and "Holy Word of God."**

The Bible is unique because it does not just contain the Word of God; *it is* the Word of God. It is able to expose the lies of satan. **The Bible is the only standard of Truth.** Nothing else can compare.

The purpose of the Bible is to restore all people to God.

To truly know God and learn who He is we must read and study the Holy Bible and pray for understanding of His Word. God gave us His Word to help us learn from those who have come before us and guide us in the right direction so we can truly live the way He intended us to.

One way God speaks to us is through His Word. Anyone who makes a genuine effort to listen to God reads and studies His Word. The Bible is not a book with "cool stories" that were made up by random people.

Truth: Everything in the Bible is real and true.

Some people absolutely refuse to believe the Bible is God's Word. They reject God and choose to believe in something else, or in some cases, anything else.

No one hates the Bible more than satan. He especially hates Genesis 3 because he does not want us to know his involvement in tempting Adam and Eve to disobey God. This was the first exposure of his cunning side and his lies. Moreover, he hates the Book of Revelation because it tells about how he loses and will be thrown into the Lake of Fire. The fact that he is the defeated enemy of Jesus is fully exposed by God's Word!

Truth: God's Word does not contradict itself.

Over time, people who reject God become blind to the truth and their hearts become hardened towards God. It is this simple: people choose to reject God, which means they choose to accept satan instead.

There is no neutral ground

How about this question, is there another satan?

Answer: No.

Are there thousands or millions of him?

Answer: No.

Has anyone ever asked you, "Which satan is real or true? This question doesn't come up too often right? It may not come up at all. Read carefully, everything created was created by God alone (Genesis 1 and Genesis 2:1-8).

There is only one true God and one true satan.

Therefore, if you are <u>not with</u> Jesus, you reject and are against Him, which means you are <u>with</u> satan. If you are <u>with</u> Jesus, you reject and are against satan.

Whose team are you on?

If you run from this question, it will not just go away. This is not a question you answer with, "Umm I think I am on..." or "Well I hope..."

Now you have full confidence in knowing where you will spend eternity, no excuses. Your eternity **will not** be left to chance. Don't let satan fool you. It is no longer an option for you to pretend where you will spend eternity.

God knows where you stand and so do you.

God has so much to offer everyone on His team. He has made the invitation, the choice is yours to make.

Wait, how can I switch teams?

Now it's time for action. **God's love** is real and requires a response from us. **Jesus did all the work but it's up to us to believe** (John 14:1). If you know or have discovered you are on satan's team, it is not too late for you. This morning, this afternoon, today, tonight is the day of your Salvation! **Your moment is Right Now.** Jesus has a purpose and a plan for your life. Yes, Jesus loves you that much and you are that important to Him!

It's time to stop living in rebellion towards God and turn away from sin. Leave worldly pleasures behind and **get off satan's team.**

On satan's team, there is no "Freedom." The idea that you can and should do whatever you want, whenever you want and rebel against God means you are a **slave** to sin. **Nothing** is worse than this. **True Freedom** comes from obeying God and doing His will. Freedom is being able to choose what to do but also what not to do.

Jesus has more in store for you than you can imagine! **Think with eternity in mind.** No matter where you are in your life or what you've done, Jesus will forgive you. He will save you but you <u>must</u> ask Him.

Joining Jesus' Team is the best decision you can make in your entire life! Romans 10:9-10 says:

"that if you confess with your mouth Jesus *as* Lord, and believe in your heart that God raised Him from the dead, you will be saved; [10] for with the heart a person believes, resulting in righteousness, and with the mouth he confesses, resulting in salvation." (NASB).

You can use the prayer below to help you invite Jesus into your heart and into your life right now.

Are you ready?

Pray this prayer aloud:

Dear God in heaven, I come to You in the name of Jesus. I acknowledge that I have sinned against You. I have been on the opposing team but I repent right now for my sins and the life that I have lived. Please forgive me. I believe that Your only begotten Son Jesus Christ shed His precious blood on the cross at Calvary and died for my sins, and I am now willing to turn from my sin.

Right now, I confess with my mouth that Jesus is the Lord of my soul and I believe in my heart that You raised Jesus from the dead. This very moment I accept Jesus Christ as my own personal Savior and according to Your Word, right now I am saved.

Thank you Jesus for your unlimited grace which has saved me from my sins. I thank you Jesus that Your grace always leads to repentance. Therefore Lord Jesus, transform my life so I may bring glory and honor to You alone and not to myself. Thank You Jesus for dying for me and giving me eternal life. Amen!

If you just said this prayer, your actions will start to show the choice you've made. This is not just for Sundays. Living for Jesus means you're "All in" everyday. You make this choice daily when you wake up. As long as you're still breathing, this is the choice you make. You want a real relationship with Jesus. You're inviting Him to transform your life and make you into the person he created you to be.

Now you need to tell someone about the choice you made, email us!

jesusisundefeated@gmail.com

Team Jesus!

You were dead in sin and on satan's losing team but now; you are alive in Christ and have joined the winning team! Angels in Heaven are rejoicing over you right now! (Luke 15:7).

Thank God for bringing you to His team instead of leaving you as you were. The Lord Jesus Christ has redeemed you for a price! The price was His death on the cross. But Jesus rose from the grave and He lives! Amen!

What to expect now

Expect Jesus to get in your business. He wants to be involved in every aspect of your life. There will be some areas that need to be cleaned up. You may lose some friends. You will break some bad habits. You will feel a strong pull to stop doing some things you were used to doing. This is natural, it means Jesus is working in your heart to make some necessary changes. Go with it!

If you're struggling with addictions, bad habits, etc., reach out and get help. Act quickly, don't wait! Be ready to fight and let Jesus lead. Jesus will work in you to set you free.

Ok so you may be wondering, "What's next?"

1. You need to find a Bible-based Church that teaches the whole Bible (let me know if you need help).

2. Pray and study God's Word <u>Every day</u>.
   You can start reading <u>in</u> the book of John,
   <u>it's</u> in the New Testament.
3. Download the "You Version" Bible app
   (it's free). There is always a Verse of the
   day to get you started in the morning. You
   can also find Awesome devotional plans;
   there are plenty of topics to choose from.
   Ask God to lead you to an area He wants
   you to work on and dive in!

If you need help, resources, a Bible, prayer or have any questions concerning something in this book, please email this address: <u>jesusisundefeated@gmail.com</u>.

May God Bless You!

Josh Burris

April 2018

<u>Special Prayer</u>

By Laura Shaffer – Prayer Warrior

Father in heaven, thank You for this one who has professed their belief in You. Pour out Your blessing on them in a tangible way so that they will sense and know Your presence and Your love. Protect them from satan who will be angry to have lost them from his team. He knows that he will never get them back!

Give them strength to live as You are calling them to live. Encourage them as they do good. Guide them in avoiding temptation and falling back into old ways. Lead them to a Bible believing church. Surround them with others who will help them grow in understanding the Bible. Open their eyes and ears to hear and see Your truth. Help them apply that truth to their lives.

Give them a desire to bring You glory through their thoughts, their words, their actions, their attitudes, and their relationships. Remind them that You are always with them and that You will never leave them or forsake them.

I pray these things in Jesus' name. Amen

End Credits

Jesus in the Bible

Has a heart of forgiveness and the power to cleanse us from all sin
(1 John 1:5-10)

Though He never sinned, He can relate to us (Hebrews 4:14-16)

Has mercy on us
(Luke 23:32-34) (Ephesians 2:4-7)

Is able to heal our infirmities
(Matthew 12:13-15)

Has compassion on us and shows us what "real love" is
(Matthew 9:35-38) (1 Corinthians 13:4-7)

Is a servant, shows us greatness is measured by how we serve others
(Mark 10:44-45)

Is patient towards us, does not want anyone to be eternally separated from Him
(2 Peter 3:8-9)

Always speaks the truth, shows us the only way to God
(John 14:6) (John 14:10) (Matthew 12:30)

Is always obedient and submissive to His Father's will
(John 17:1-5) (Matthew 26:38-39)

Was tortured, crucified, died to pay for our sins, rose
from the dead and appeared to the disciples and others,
and ascended into heaven (Yes Jesus is alive!) Made
Salvation possible
(Luke 23:13-46) (Luke 24)

Is full of grace and truth
(John 1:14)

Gives everlasting life and will return to receive all those
who believe!
(John 3:16-21) (John 14:1-3)

satan in the Bible

An angel created by God, was covered in "every precious stone", disobeyed and rebelled against God and was cast out of heaven
(Ezekiel 28:13-15) (Revelation 12:7-12)

Defies God and despises truth
(John 8:42-47)

Attempts to hide the actual truth about God, blinds the minds of those who don't believe
(2 Corinthians 4:3-4) (Galatians 1:6-7)

Is our adversary, prowls around like a Lion seeking whoever he can "devour"
(1 Peter 5:8)

Commander of demons (fallen angels who follow satan)
(Ephesians 6:12)

Controls those outside of God's protection
(Ephesians 2:1-3)

His power and authority is limited
(Job 1:6-12)

Disguises himself as "an angel of light" (An imposter)
(2 Corinthians 11:14-15)

Is a thief who comes only to kill, steal and destroy us
(John 10:10)

Arrogant and Foolish, Even tempted Jesus to sin, failed
miserably, cannot defeat Jesus
(Matthew 4:1-11)

Looks for an "opportune time" to tempt us, wants to destroy us
(Luke 4:13)

Will spend eternity in the Lake of Fire and Brimstone
(Revelation 20:10)

Jesus Is...

Perfect	Deliverer	Trustworthy	Alive
Holy	Restoring	Immune	Active
Righteous	Moving	Responsive	Amazing
Love	Fulfilling	Honorable	Inspiring
Kind	Distinctive	Honored	Abundant
A Good Father	Comforting	Legitimate	Rich
Our Help	Our Provider	Reliable	Adequate
Our Protector	Our Shepherd	Good	Pure
Purifying	Celebrated	Modest	Freeing
Worshipped	Real	Caring	Liberating
Praised	Wholesome	Powerful	Preserving
Glorified	Safe haven	Almighty	Reproving
Famous	Beneficial	Compassionate	Courageous
Renowned	Excellent	Forgiving	Victorious
Served	Eminent	Empowering	Credited
Needed	Prominent	Discerning	Historical
Sought	Remarkable	Overwhelming	Proven
Living	Extraordinary	All Consuming	Incorruptible
Beautiful	Supernatural	Cleansing	Unfailing
Required	Miraculous	Healer	Infallible
Omnipotent	Omnipresent	Omniscient	Eternal

Just to name a few...

satan is...

The opponent of God, of believers and all that is right and good

The devil, the serpent, the evil one, the prince of this world

The accuser, the tempter, the proud one (arrogant)

The slanderer, Father of lies, Greatest deceiver

The rebel and lawless one, appears as an "angel of light"

A perverter and distorter of the Truth

The god of this world/age, the prince of the power of the air

The spirit who works in the sons of disobedience

Lucifer, son of the morning

Best known for: his hatred for Christ and for God's people, his limited power and authority, his popularity among non-believers, his ability to deceive, his blasphemy against God and war against believers

ABOUT THE AUTHOR

Josh Burris (aka JB) majored in Speech Communications and Media Relations at Colorado State University. This allowed him to experience writing in a variety of ways but Josh never planned to be an author. In 2016, Josh had conversations with various people at work and through playing sports. He began to see there was a need to share the truth with people about who Jesus really is. This also meant it would be important to share the truth about who satan really is and expose his plan to keep people from knowing the truth.

Later in 2016, Josh learned about a new show airing on Fox, *Lucifer*, a ridiculous fabrication of satan. Josh could see satan's idiotic attempt to reinvent himself to the world through this foolish TV series. After asking God what he should do, Josh received his answer, **"Share the truth."** This book was written to reveal the truth about satan (aka the devil, formerly lucifer) and more importantly to share the good news, the truth about who Jesus *really* is! Josh's writing style is clear and to the point. The length of the book is shorter than most but each page reveals the *Real* truth.

Bonus Features

JESUS vs satan Soundtrack

It is highly encouraged that all music be purchased so you can take it wherever you go and support
the artists. Listen often! Music should be available on
Google play and iTunes.

If you need lyrics email me. The most important
aspect of this music are the lyrics, please pay attention to
them! Even if you don't like the music, at least give the
lyrics a read. A Huge Thank You to All these Artists
who live for Jesus! Check it out below:

Josh Burris's Blog

Truth Music is Here

Once the page loads, scroll down and click on "JESUS
vs satan Soundtrack" please visit:

https://truthmusicalways.wordpress.com

If you would like a YouTube link, please email
jesusisundefeated@gmail.com

Team JESUS Apparel

Do you enjoy wearing apparel of your favorite sports teams? Well now, you can wear special apparel that represents something much more important than being a sports fan.

Being a Believer on Jesus' Team!

Wristbands and t-shirts!

Get ready to represent Jesus by the way you live AND by what you wear!

Please Email to: jesusisundefeated@gmail.com for more information!

Must See Movies!
God's Not Dead
Do You Believe?
War Room
The Case for Christ
Courageous
Fireproof
Facing the Giants
The Encounter

Videos that help explain the Bible

The Bible Project (YouTube)

Life Ticket (See the next page)

Every individual must have their **own Life ticket.**

Only Jesus can Redeem the "You PAY" **ticket.** If you have this ticket, see the "Wait, how can I switch teams?" section.

Take this with you! Laminate it and carry it in your wallet or purse, frame it, etc. Be sure to fill in the "Date Received" first. This is the date you received Salvation and joined Jesus' Team!

Eternal Life
Theatres
Heaven

Auditorium **33**

JESUS – Savior of the World
Rated – TR
$Price: JESUS PAID
ADMIT ONE – Jesus's Team
Date Received:
Promise Validated

ETERNAL DEATH
Theatres
Lake of Fire

Auditorium **13**

satan – master of deception
Rated – TR
$Price: YOU PAY
ADMIT ONE – satan's team
Date Received: Your DOB
Deceived by Lies